ENJOY YOUR FREEDOM

by Warren W. Wiersbe
Associate Bible Teacher
Back to the Bible Broadcast

A
BACK TO THE BIBLE
PUBLICATION

Back to the Bible

Lincoln, Nebraska 68501

65,000 printed to date—1983
(5-1911—65M—63)
ISBN 0-8474-6507-1

Cover photo by PTO Productions.

All Scripture quotations are from *The New Scofield Reference Bible.*

Printed in the United States of America

Contents

Chapter 1

What Is Freedom?

While window-shopping one day, I saw a T-shirt with beautiful butterflies printed on it. The lettering on the T-shirt read: "Butterflies are free!" Of course, butterflies are free! *They are free to be butterflies,* but they certainly aren't free to fly to the moon!

Our world is concerned about freedom, but very few people ask, "What really is freedom?" or, "If I did have freedom, how would I use it?" Here is what the Lord Jesus Christ had to say about freedom: "As he spoke these words, many believed on him. Then said Jesus to those Jews who believed on him, If ye continue in my word, then are ye my disciples indeed; and ye shall know the truth, and the truth shall make you free. They answered him, We are Abraham's seed, and were never in bondage to any man. How sayest thou, Ye shall be made free? Jesus answered them, Verily, verily, I say unto you, Whosoever committeth sin is the servant of sin. And the servant abideth not in the house forever; but the Son abideth ever. If the Son, therefore, shall make you free, ye shall be free indeed" (John 8:30-36).

5

The people to whom Jesus was speaking were confused about freedom. Imagine a Jew's saying, "We have never been in bondage to any man!" When you read Old Testament history, you find that the Jewish nation was often in bondage because God had to discipline them. In fact, at the very hour our Lord was speaking, the Jewish nation was under the heel of the Roman government!

Many people do not understand freedom. If you want to understand and enjoy freedom, you must understand the three affirmations that the Lord Jesus Christ made in this passage of Scripture: (1) God's purpose for man is freedom; (2) God's method for freedom is truth; and (3) God's revelation of truth is Jesus Christ.

God's Purpose for Man

God's purpose for man is freedom. What is freedom? Many people think that freedom is the absence of restraint, but that could lead to anarchy. Suppose we had no laws telling us on what side of the highway to drive. Suppose we had no regulations governing such things as medicine or money. Suppose we were able to do whatever we wanted to do. The world would be filled with chaos! Freedom is not the absence of restraint, nor is freedom doing whatever you please. That could be the greatest kind of selfish bondage. *Freedom is the privilege and power to become all that God wants you to become. Freedom is the opportunity to fulfill your potential to the glory of God.*

You were born with a tremendous potential. When you were born again through faith in Jesus Christ, God added spiritual gifts to your natural talents. God surrounds you with opportunity. You and I are free in Jesus Christ, not to do whatever we want but to be all that God wants us to be. Freedom is the opportunity to fulfill your potential to the glory of God.

You were made in the image of God. God made you to be free. When God put the first man and woman in the garden, He gave them freedom— freedom that was governed by regulation, freedom that was hedged in by protective law. They were free to work for God. They were free to walk with God. But they were not free to disobey God so that they might have their own way. Creation says to me, "God made you to be free." We are made in the image of God to enjoy the freedom that He has made for us.

The Bible is a book of freedom. Beginning with the Exodus, when God set His people free, all the way through to the Book of the Revelation, the emphasis is on freedom. Whenever the nation of Israel sinned, they found themselves in bondage. Whenever they obeyed God, they found themselves enjoying freedom. The Bible is a book of freedom. The cross speaks of freedom. The Holy City, the New Jerusalem, speaks of freedom. Every word in the New Testament pointing to Jesus Christ emphasizes freedom. Freedom begins with salvation, freedom begins with trusting Jesus Christ as your Saviour.

Jesus said that whoever commits sin is the servant of sin (John 8:34). That verb means "is in the habit of practicing sin." In other words, when you and I repeatedly, continually disobey God, that isn't freedom; that's the worst kind of bondage. When you trust Jesus Christ as your Saviour, you have freedom *from* the guilt, the punishment, the judgment of sin. You have freedom *in* walking with the Lord, in the Spirit, overcoming the power of sin. And you have freedom *to* become all that God wants you to become. You have freedom to grow, to develop your full potential and become like the Lord Jesus Christ. God's purpose for man is freedom.

God's Method for Freedom

God's method for freedom is truth. Two forces are at work in this world today—the force that comes from heaven and the force that comes from hell. The power of God works through truth, and the power of the Devil works through lies. Satan is the liar. Jesus made that very clear in John 8:44: "Ye are of your father the devil, and the lusts of your father ye will do. He was a murderer from the beginning, and abode not in the truth, because there is no truth in him. When he speaketh a lie, he speaketh of his own; for he is a liar, and the father of it."

Satan uses lies to bring you into bondage, and that bondage leads to destruction; but God uses truth to bring you into freedom, and that freedom leads to fulfillment. In Genesis 3 Satan said to our

8

first parents, "Yea, hath God said?" (v. 1) and then he promised them, "Ye shall be as God" (v. 5). Satan was offering them freedom without responsibility, freedom without consequences, *and there can be no such thing.* Satan's lie is "Ye shall be as God," and that is the lie that rules the world today. Man is his own God. The world today is worshiping "the creature more than the Creator" (Rom. 1:25). Man no longer looks at himself as a creature who must be obedient to God. Man looks at himself as the creator. Man is now his own God! God's purpose for man is freedom, and God's method for freedom is truth.

Truth has been given to us in three different ways. In John 14:6 Jesus said, "I am . . . the truth." Jesus is the truth. This is why He claimed in John 8:36, "If the Son, therefore, shall make you free, ye shall be free indeed." This ties in with verse 32, "And ye shall know the truth, and the truth shall make you free." When you know Jesus Christ, you know God's living truth, and that truth sets you free.

The Word of God is truth. In John 17:17 our Lord said, "Sanctify them through thy truth; thy word is truth." This is why Jesus said in John 8:31,32, "If ye continue in my word, then are ye my disciples indeed; and ye shall know the truth, and the truth shall make you free." The Word of God is the truth of God. The Word of God also exposes the Devil's lies. When you and I have a personal relationship with the Son of God, we have truth. When we spend time studying and meditating on the Word of God, we have truth.

9

In I John 5:6, we are told that the Spirit is the truth. The Spirit of God gave us the Word of God. The Word of God is inspired by the Holy Spirit. The Holy Spirit of God teaches us the truth of the Word of God. "Where the Spirit of the Lord is, there is liberty" (II Cor. 3:17). When the Spirit of God reveals the Son of God in the Word of God, we experience the freedom of God. God's method for freedom is truth. But let me warn you. Satan is at work with his lies, and Satan wants you to believe his lies. When you believe the truth and obey it, you experience freedom. When you believe the Devil's lies and obey them, then you experience bondage. God's purpose for man is freedom, and God's method for freedom is truth.

God's Revelation of Truth

Third, *God's revelation of truth is Jesus Christ.* "If the Son, therefore, shall make you free, ye shall be free indeed" (John 8:36). The Lord Jesus Christ could not make us free unless He were free Himself. When you read the four Gospels, you see the experience of Jesus Christ here on earth, and He experienced freedom. He came to a nation that was under political bondage, but even more than that, it was under *spiritual* and *religious* bondage. The Pharisees had added so many traditions to the Word of God that the people were shackled. A yoke was put on the people that made it difficult for them to enjoy God. The Lord Jesus Christ was free from legalism. You don't see Him bowing down to the traditions of men. He was free from fear. He slept in a boat in the midst of a storm! He went to Calvary without fear. You don't see the Lord Jesus Christ in bondage to any person or system because He was free. "If the Son, therefore, shall make you free, ye shall be free indeed" (v. 36).

The better you know the Lord Jesus Christ, the more freedom you are going to enjoy. Our responsibility is to know Him. How do you get to know Him? Through the Word of God. "Ye shall know the truth, and the truth shall make you free" (v. 32). Do you spend time daily in the Word of God? Are you studying the Word of God? Are you learning the Word of God? Have you discovered that the Word of God is your key to freedom? Get to *know* Him, and that word "know" doesn't simply mean to know intellectually. It means to have a living relationship with Him. Know Him. Trust Him. "If ye continue in my word, then are ye my disciples indeed" (v. 31). Yield to the Word of God. Try to do all that God wants you to do. It's important, very important, for the Word of God to fill our hearts and minds. We must know Him and we must trust Him.

We must love Him. "If God were your Father, ye would love me; for I proceeded forth and came from God; neither came I of myself, but he sent me" (v. 42). You see, the better we know Him, the more we trust Him. And the better we know Him, the more we love Him.

We should obey Christ. "If a man keep my saying, he shall never see death" (v. 51). That's an amazing statement, isn't it? Many Christians have died, but

11

death was not an enemy. Death did not devour them or destroy them. Death was simply the open door that led to glory. Our responsibility is to know Jesus Christ better, to trust Him, to love Him and to obey Him. When we have this living relationship with Jesus Christ, we begin to experience more and more of His freedom. This freedom we enjoy will be seen in our thinking, our speaking, our behaving. We experience joyful freedom, and we become more like the Lord Jesus Christ.

Now the interesting thing is this: The more you become like the Lord Jesus Christ, the more it releases your potential. We have yet to see what God can do in our lives! You may think you have no gifts or abilities. You may think there are no opportunities for you. You may be discouraged. But the more you become like Jesus Christ, the more you experience freedom. And the more freedom you experience, the more you release your own potential. Oh, the wonderful power and potential that God has put within you! *Freedom is life controlled by truth and motivated by love.* Bondage is life controlled by lies and motivated by selfishness. Freedom is the result of a living relationship with Jesus Christ—walking with Him, talking with Him and learning from Him.

If you have never trusted Christ as your Saviour, I would appeal to you to do so. Yield your life to Him. If you are already a Christian, you may be saying, "I don't want to be yielded to Christ. I want to live my own life." That's the worst kind of bondage. You see, sin's freedom is bondage, but bondage to Jesus

Christ is true freedom. I want your life to be controlled by truth and motivated by love because, "If the Son, therefore, shall make you free, ye shall be free indeed" (v. 36).

Chapter 2

False Freedom

Christian freedom is a life controlled by truth and motivated by love. It's the result of a growing relationship with Jesus Christ, who is the truth, and with the Word of God, and with the Holy Spirit of God, who is the Spirit of truth. But there is a false freedom in the world today, a freedom that comes not from heaven but from hell. Those who practice this false freedom have a life that is controlled by lies and motivated by lust.

This false freedom is described in II Peter 2. "But there were false prophets also among the people, even as there shall be false teachers among you, who secretly shall bring in destructive heresies, even denying the Lord that bought them, and bring upon themselves swift destruction. And many shall follow their pernicious ways, by reason of whom the way of truth shall be evil spoken of. And through covetousness shall they, with feigned words, make merchandise of you; whose judgment now for a long time lingereth not, and their destruction slumbereth not" (vv. 1-3).

14

"These are wells without water, clouds that are carried with a tempest, to whom the mist of darkness is reserved forever. For when they speak great swelling words of vanity, they allure through the lusts of the flesh, through much wantonness, those that are just escaping from them who live in error. While they promise them liberty, they themselves are the servants of corruption; for of whom a man is overcome, of the same is he brought in bondage. For if, after they have escaped the pollutions of the world through the knowledge of the Lord and Savior, Jesus Christ, they are again entangled in it, and overcome, the latter end is worse with them than the beginning. For it had been better for them not to have known the way of righteousness than, after they have known it, to turn from the holy commandment delivered unto them. But it has happened unto them according to the true proverb, The dog is turned to his own vomit again; and the sow that was washed, to her wallowing in the mire" (vv. 17-22).

This is not a very beautiful picture is it? But it is one we need to look at because it contains a number of warnings we need to heed. These false teachers go after young Christians. Notice verse 18: "They allure through the lusts of the flesh, through much wantonness, those that are just escaping from them who live in error." They go after new believers and seek to lead them into a false freedom that turns into terrible bondage. Peter urged us to avoid this false freedom, and he gave three reasons why this freedom is dangerous.

15

Where False Freedom Comes From

False freedom is dangerous because of where it comes from.

It comes from false teachers. Wherever you find the true, you find the false. Wherever you find the genuine, you will find the counterfeit. There were false prophets among the people of Israel, and there are going to be false teachers among Christians today. These teachers claim to believe in the Lord and follow the Word of God, and yet they so twist the Word of God and so misapply the Word of God that they lead people into bondage.

Notice what Peter said about these teachers, for he identified them accurately. In verse 1 these false teachers secretly introduce destructive heresies. They are not honest. They work in an underhanded way, and they deny the very Lord who died for them. This doesn't mean that these false teachers are saved. In fact, at the end of this chapter we find that they are not sheep; they are dogs and sows who have been washed, but they have never been changed into sheep. They are counterfeit. They are pretenders.

Verse 10 says that these people despise authority: "But chiefly them that walk after the flesh and the lust of uncleanness, and despise government. Presumptuous are they; self-willed, they are not afraid to speak evil of dignities." They are proud, boastful people who think they are the only ones who are right. They deny the Lord and despise authority, and they defile everything they touch.

They walk in the lust of uncleanness, according to II Peter 2:10. Throughout II Peter 2 this description is given of uncleanness, perniciousness, wickedness and evil. Of course, the worst part is that they are deceived and that they are deceivers. They deceive others because they are deceived themselves. It's a tragic picture.

According to verse 3, they use "feigned words." The Greek word translated "feigned" (*plastos*) is the word from which we get the English word "plastic." What are plastic words? They are words that can be twisted around to mean anything. The false teachers use our vocabulary but not our dictionary. When they talk about freedom or salvation or sin, they are not defining those words the way we do. They have plastic words.

"They . . . make merchandise of you," says verse 3. They're just out to make money! In fact, verses 14 and 18 tell me that they entice people. They beguile and allure unstable souls. They "speak great swelling words of vanity." These people promote their lies to make merchandise of young Christians and lead them astray. In verse 17 he compared them to wells without water and to clouds that promise rain but don't give any. Verse 13 says, in effect, "They are spots in your love feasts," blemishes in the Body of the believers. They pretend to be Christians, but all they want to do is use religion as a means of making money and leading people into sin.

Beware of this false freedom because of where it comes from. It comes from false teachers who despise the authority of the Word of God, who will

17

defile you, who will deceive you. They will lead you into depravity. They will entice you and allure you with their plastic words, their arrogant words, their empty words. They are religious racketeers.

What False Freedom Offers

Beware of this false freedom, not only because of where it comes from *but also because of what it offers.*

Freedom Without Responsibility

What are they offering to people? They are offering them *freedom without responsibility,* and that's a dangerous thing. Whatever gives you freedom without adding to your self-control will lead you into bondage and destruction. The Prodigal Son wanted freedom, but he didn't want responsibility. There can be no true freedom without responsibility. Unearned freedom is a dangerous, destructive thing. This is what Satan offered our first parents in the Garden of Eden—freedom without responsibility. "Why should you listen to God? Has God said that you shall not eat of this tree? Exercise your freedom. You can get away with it!" (see Gen. 3:1,4,5). Beware of anyone who offers you freedom without responsibility.

Freedom Without Reckoning

They also offer *freedom without reckoning.* They say there will not be any judgment. "You're not going to face God and have to answer for this!" Sometimes they even use the Bible to teach their pernicious false doctrines. They say something like this: "After all, we live by grace, don't we? We're saved by grace, and we're not under Law. Therefore, we can live any way we please." Paul answered that in Romans 6:1,2: "What shall we say then? Shall we continue in sin, that grace may abound? God forbid."

Freedom Without Repercussions

False grace leads to false freedom, and this freedom will have a day of reckoning. So they're offering freedom without responsibility, and they're offering freedom without reckoning. They are also offering *freedom without repercussions*. They're saying, "Oh, you can go out and do this, and there won't be any consequences. You can get away with it!" But you *can't* get away with it. "The wages of sin is death" (Rom. 6:23), and "the soul that sinneth, it shall die" (Ezek. 18:4). Anyone who deliberately, repeatedly, lovingly, willingly lives in sin is proving he has never been born again.

Freedom Without Recession

They also offer *freedom without any recession*. They're saying, "This freedom gets better and better. As you enjoy sin, it gets better and better." But sin *doesn't* get better and better! It gets worse! Sin begins with a great deal of pleasure and ends with pain. Those who live in sin are in terrible bondage. They must have more and more sin, and yet they enjoy it less and less. Sin enslaves those who practice it.

19

Where False Freedom Leads

Peter gave us a third reason why we should avoid this false freedom—not only because of where it comes from and because of what it offers but *because of what it leads to.*

What does it lead to? Bondage. In II Peter 2:19 he said, "While they promised them liberty, they themselves are the servants of corruption; for of whom a man is overcome, of the same is he brought in bondage." They are entangled and overcome (v. 20). They want to use this doctrine of false freedom to get you into their cult, into their group, so they can make merchandise of you. They rob you. They exploit you. They ruin you. And it leads to bondage and to judgment.

I do not believe that any Christian will ever face judgment. "There is, therefore, now no condemnation to them who are in Christ Jesus" (Rom. 8:1). But he may face terrible discipline in this life. In my ministry, I have met some people who have believed these false doctrines and have gotten into what they thought was freedom, and how God had to chasten them and discipline them! These false teachers bring upon themselves "swift destruction" (II Pet. 2:1). They are reserved "unto the day of judgment" (v. 9). It is dangerous to get into false freedom because it leads to heartache, bondage and discipline.

Peter illustrated this judgment by pointing to the angels (v. 4). Satan caused the fall of the angels, and where did they end up? In freedom? No! They ended up in bondage, in the chains of darkness.

In verse 5 he mentioned the world before the flood. People were living in freedom. They were enjoying life and ignoring God. Then judgment came! In verses 6-8 he pointed to Sodom and Gomorrah where people lived in the filthiness of the flesh. I don't have to elaborate on the horrible sins of Sodom and Gomorrah. Did those sins lead to freedom? They led to bondage! In verse 4 Satan led the angels astray. In verse 5 we have the world rejecting God. In verses 6-8 we have Sodom and Gommorah, the flesh. In these verses we see the world, the flesh and the Devil. If you live for the world, the flesh and the Devil, you are living in a false freedom. It will only lead to bondage, discipline and destruction.

Paul sounded the right note in Galatians 5:13: "For, brethren, ye have been called unto liberty; only use not liberty for an occasion to the flesh, but by love serve one another." This is the way we are supposed to live. True freedom is life controlled by truth and motivated by love. If you want to enjoy real freedom, serve other people in love. Sin's freedom is bondage, but bondage to Christ is true freedom. We should not use our liberty as an excuse to sin.

I want to warn you about this false freedom. Young Christians who have not yet been grounded in the Word of God need to be warned against those who want to make merchandise of them. The false teacher says, "You don't want to listen to the Word of God! You don't want to be identified with that

21

Bible-preaching church! Come into our group. We have true freedom! You can enjoy the things of the world, the flesh and the Devil, and you don't have to worry about responsibility or reckoning or repercussions!" They promise that life will get better and better, but in reality it will get worse and worse, and you will experience terrible chastening from the Lord. It is a dangerous thing to get involved in false freedom. Jesus said, "If the Son, therefore, shall make you free, ye shall be free indeed" (John 8:36). True freedom is life controlled by truth and motivated by love.

Are you involved in some false group, believing some false doctrine? Beware because all that is false will one day be cast into hell! Only what is true shall last. "And ye shall know the truth, and the truth shall make you free" (v. 32).

Chapter 3

Freedom From Law

What does it mean to be free from the Law? "Stand fast, therefore, in the liberty with which Christ hath made us free, and be not entangled again with the yoke of bondage" (Gal. 5:1). What is freedom from the Law as far as the Christian is concerned? It certainly does not mean that Christians are permitted to be lawless. Rather it means that our relationship to God is not based on Law but on grace.

Perhaps the best way to understand our freedom from the Law is to consider seven different pictures of the Law given to us in the New Testament. Each of these pictures tells us why the Law was given, what the Lord Jesus Christ did and then what we must do in our relationship to Christ and to the Law.

The Law As a Yoke

In Galatians 5:1 we have the first picture of the Law: The Law is compared to *a yoke.* "Stand fast, therefore, in the liberty with which Christ hath made us free, and be not entangled again with the yoke of bondage." In Acts 15:10 we read: "Now,

23

therefore, why put God to the test, to put a yoke upon the neck of the disciples, which neither our fathers nor we were able to bear?" The great question debated in Acts 15 was "Must a Gentile become a Jew to become a Christian?" Some of the legalists in the church said, "Yes, the Gentiles must put themselves under the Law," but the conclusion reached was "No, we must not put people under that yoke."

Why is the Law compared to a yoke? Who uses a yoke? Yokes are used with animals. The Law was given as a yoke to control us. Some tell us that people are basically good, that their problem is really the environment or the economy or education. No, man is basically a sinner. He has an animal nature, and that nature must be kept under control. One reason why God gave the Law was to control man. The Law never changes anybody; and in spite of the fact that we do have laws today, people still live like animals! But think of what the world would be like if there were no laws. As long as I am driving on the right side of the street, obeying the speed limit and doing what the law tells me to do, I have the freedom to drive. If I decide I want to drive on the wrong side of the street at twice the speed limit, I rob myself of freedom, and I need a yoke to control me. The Law was given to help control the animal nature in man. God revealed His righteous judgments in the Law, and God warned man in the Law. But man still rebels against God.

The Lord Jesus Christ not only bore the yoke of the Law, but He bore the sins of the world on the cross. He fulfilled the Law. Galatians 5:1 tells us that we have been set free by the Lord Jesus Christ. When you're wearing a yoke, you are not standing straight on your feet. In order to wear a yoke, you would have to get down on all fours. The yoke burdens you, galls you, irritates you. The yoke is against you, but that yoke helps to control you.

Jesus Christ bore the curse of the Law when He died on the cross. Galatians 3:13 says, "Christ hath redeemed us from the curse of the law, being made a curse for us; for it is written, Cursed is everyone that hangeth on a tree." Instead of wearing the yoke of the Law, we Christians wear the wonderful yoke of Jesus Christ. He said in Matthew 11:28-30, "Come unto me, all ye that labor and are heavy laden, and I will give you rest. Take my yoke upon you, and learn of me; for I am meek and lowly in heart, and ye shall find rest unto your souls. For my yoke is easy, and my burden is light."

In other words, you and I as Christians have exchanged the *external* yoke of legalism for the *internal* yoke of love. We are related to Jesus Christ through a living, loving relationship, and we don't mind wearing His yoke because it is tailor-made for us. It is fitted to us. It is an easy yoke, and it helps us to be free. That is remarkable, isn't it? The yoke of the Law puts a person under bondage, but the yoke of Jesus Christ sets a person free. The yoke of the Law brought restlessness and agony, but the yoke of Jesus Christ brings rest to our souls. If you are a Christian, you are no longer to wear a yoke of the Law. That is bondage. Jesus bore your sins on the cross. Jesus fulfilled the righteous demands of the Law. Jesus was made a curse for you on the tree. Therefore, take His yoke, learn of Him, and enjoy the rest that He alone can give.

The Law As a Guardian

The second picture of the Law is in Galatians 4:1-5. The Law is compared to *a guardian.* "Now I say that the heir, as long as he is a child, differeth nothing from a servant, though he be lord of all, but is under tutors and governors [guardians and stewards] until the time appointed of the father. Even so we, when we were children, were in bondage under the elements of the world. But, when the fullness of the time was come, God sent forth his Son, made of a woman, made under the law, to redeem them that were under the law, that we might receive the adoption of sons."

When Israel was called by God, the nation was like a nation of children. They were spiritually immature. You need guardians, tutors and governors to take care of little children. In the Greek and Roman homes, slaves cared for the immature children. They took them to school and back and watched over them. The Law was like a guardian that watched over Israel during its immaturity.

When our children were small, we had to guard them. We had to have rules and regulations. Some things were very definitely off limits to our children. We would say, "Now, don't go near the highway" or "Don't go near the basement stairs" or "Don't leave the basement door open." Little children need guardians because they are immature and lack the discernment of adults.

When the Jewish nation came to its time of maturity, then the Saviour, their Messiah, was sent to them. God wanted to usher them into a new relationship. He wanted to redeem them from the Law and give them the position of adult sons. "But, when the fullness of the time was come [the maturity of the nation], God sent forth his Son, made of a woman, made under the law, to redeem them that were under the law, that we might receive the adoption of sons" (vv. 4,5). The word "adoption" refers to "an adult standing in the family." Adults do not need guardians. Adults do not need servants and tutors to direct, protect and care for them. Anyone who puts himself under the Law is saying, "I want to be immature." It is impossible to mature if you put yourself under Law.

Christ has redeemed us from the Law. We now have a position in the family as adult sons, not as little children. We no longer need rules and regulations on the outside because we have the life of God on the inside. Galatians 4:6,7 says, "Because ye are sons, God hath sent forth the Spirit of his Son into your hearts, crying, Abba, Father. Wherefore, thou art no more a servant, but a son; and if a son, then an heir of God through Christ."

Jesus Christ died on the cross, rose again and went back to heaven. He sent the Holy Spirit, and the Holy Spirit now lives in believers. We have the Spirit of God within; so we do not need the Law as a tutor, or a governor, on the outside. The Lord Jesus

27

Christ has given us an adult standing in the family. It is a marvelous thing to know that you have an adult standing before God! God is not treating you like a little child. He has put His Spirit within you, and the Holy Spirit says, "Abba, Father." Our relationship to God is not that of a servant obeying laws; it is that of a son showing love, respect and obedience.

The Law As a Slave Girl

In Galatians 4:21-31 is a third picture of the Law. The Law is pictured as *a slave girl*. This is the story of Abraham and Hagar from Genesis 16. You remember that Abraham got impatient waiting for his son to be born. Sarah suggested that Abraham take Hagar, her slave girl, as his wife. He did. A child, Ishmael, was born who turned out to be a real problem. When Isaac was born, a few years later, Ishmael persecuted Isaac and made trouble in the home. God said to Abraham, "Cast out the bondwoman and her son" (Gal. 4:30). The contrast here is between Sarah and Hagar: Sarah was a free woman, but Hagar was a slave. Sarah represents the heavenly Jerusalem, but Hagar represents the earthly Jerusalem in bondage.

Notice Galatians 4:24-26: "Which things are an allegory [a story that has hidden spiritual meaning]; for these are the two covenants: the one from the Mount Sinai, bearing children for bondage, who is Hagar. For this Hagar is Mount Sinai in Arabia, and answereth to Jerusalem which now is, and is in bondage with her children. But Jerusalem which is above is free, which is the mother of us all." Hagar

28

represents the earthly Jerusalem, the covenant of Law. Sarah represents the heavenly Jerusalem, the covenant of grace. Isaac was born a free son, but Ishmael was born a slave. Isaac represents our birth in the Spirit, and Ishmael represents our birth in the flesh.

When I was born the first time, I was born with a sinful nature and, like Ishmael, was a rebel, a troublemaker. When I was born again, I was born with a new nature (like the birth of Isaac) through the power of God. This new nature enables me to obey the Lord.

What did God say to Abraham? Galatians 4:30 says, "Cast out the bondwoman and her son; for the son of the bondwoman shall not be heir with the son of the freewoman." You cannot inherit anything through the Law. The only way to inherit anything from God is to be born into His family, and you cannot be born into His family through the Law. You must be born into the family through the power of the Holy Spirit. Abraham represents faith, and Sarah represents grace. Isaac, their son, was born by grace through faith. Abraham, Sarah, Isaac— these three represent the spiritual life. Hagar and Ishmael represent the old life, the life of bondage under Law. We are not the children of the bondwoman but of the free woman. Your mother (spiritually) is not Hagar. The Law did not give you birth. The Spirit of God gave you your birth. Your mother, so to speak, is Sarah, the heavenly Jerusalem. You were born from above, born after the Spirit, born free, not born into bondage. So the only thing we can do is cast out the bondwoman and her son.

When the Law goes, the flesh has to go because "the strength of sin is the law" (I Cor. 15:56). When the Law says, "Don't do this!" my old nature says, "I'm going to do it!" When the Law says, "You'd better do that!" I say, "Oh, no I won't!" The old nature *knows* no law, but the new nature *needs* no law. We are not under the bondage of the Law. We were not born as slave children. We were born free. We were born under grace, and therefore, we are no longer under the bondage of the Law.

Abraham was never supposed to marry Hagar. God never married the Law to grace. The Law has its function. It tells me I need grace, convicts me of sin and tells me that God is righteous and that sin leads to death. But Abraham was never supposed to marry Hagar, and so God said, "Cast out the bondwoman and her son" (Gal. 4:30). We are not under the yoke of the Law. We are wearing the yoke of Christ. We no longer need guardians or baby-sitters because we have the Spirit within. We are adult sons in the family. We are not related to the slave girl, Hagar. We are free because we have been born again by the Spirit of the living God.

Chapter 4

Freedom From Law (cont.)

The New Testament gives us seven pictures of the Law. We have already considered three of them.

The Law As a Bond of Indebtedness

In Colossians 2:14 we have the fourth picture of the Law: *the bond of indebtedness.* If you have ever owed anybody money, you know something about the bond of indebtedness. Paul was writing about the work of Jesus Christ on the cross: "Blotting out the handwriting of ordinances that was against us, which was contrary to us, and took it out of the way, nailing it to his cross." We were in debt to the Law.

The Law was against us. You must remember that the Law was not given to save people. It was given to show people they needed to be saved. The Law was against us because it revealed sin. It was against us because it revealed the holy and righteous judgments of God. The Law was not only against us, but it was also contrary to us. This takes us a step further, doesn't it? We *could not* obey it. No matter how much we try, we cannot obey the Law.

righteousness is like filthy rags (see Isa. 64:6). We cannot begin to conform to the standards of God. So what did Jesus do? He paid the debt for us. He blotted out the handwriting of ordinances (Col. 2:14). In other words, He cancelled the debt. In Paul's day legal documents were written on parchment and vellum. You could use water or some other fluid to erase, expunge, wash away completely the writing that was on the document.

When Jesus died for us on the cross, He not only washed away the writing on the document, but He also nailed the document to His cross. He took it out of the way. Some people today want to put the Law back into the center of their lives. When Jesus died on the cross, He tore the veil of the temple in two. This signified that there was no longer any division between man and God. We can come through the blood of Jesus Christ to our Father in heaven. The way is open. All of the ceremonies have been fulfilled, every demand of the Law has been met, every debt has been paid. He also knocked down the middle wall of partition between Jew and Gentile (see Eph. 2:14). There are no more racial distinctions. The Law that was given to the Jews was never given to the Gentiles. That racial distinction has been completely erased.

Jesus blotted out the handwriting of ordinances that was against us. We are no longer in debt! He has taken it out of the way. The Law is no longer the central thing in our lives. What is the central thing? The cross. Paul said, "God forbid that I should glory, except in the cross of our Lord Jesus Christ"

(Gal. 6:14). Why do we obey God? Because of the Law that is hanging over our head? No. *Because of a life that is within our heart.* Our debt, or responsibility, is not to fulfill the Law. Our debt is to love. Romans 13:8 says, "Owe no man any thing, but to love one another; for he that loveth another hath fulfilled the law." Colossians 2:14 affirms that the bond of indebtedness has been erased and has been nailed to the cross, and therefore, we owe no debt to the Law. Does this mean we are lawless? Of course not! It means that the Law is now written in our hearts because we have the Holy Spirit within. A new nature within gives us the desire and the power to obey God and to live up to the righteous standards of the Law.

The Law As a Shadow

As we continue in Colossians 2, we discover a fifth picture of the Law: *the shadows.* Colossians 2:16,17 says, "Let no man, therefore, judge you in food, or in drink, or in respect of a feast day, or of the new moon, or of a sabbath day, which are a shadow of things to come; but the body is of Christ."

The problem in Colossae was this: The Christians were being taught by false teachers who mixed Law and grace. They taught that believers had to obey the Old Testament dietary laws and observe the yearly feasts. Paul wrote, in effect: "Don't let them judge you in respect to a holy day (the annual feasts) or the new moon (the monthly celebration) or the Sabbath Day (the weekly celebration)"

34

(v. 16). All of these special days were a part of the "shadow of things to come" (v. 17).

The same truth is taught in Hebrew 10:1: "For the law, having a shadow of good things to come and not the very image of the things, can never with those sacrifices which they offered year by year continually make those who come to it perfect." The Law is simply a shadow. Heavenly, spiritual realities are pictured in earthly, physical copies. The tabernacle was a copy of God's tabernacle in heaven. The sacrifices were a copy of the sacrifice of Jesus Christ. When you put yourself under the Law, you are going from the light into the shadow. When you put yourself under the Law, you are exchanging the reality for the copy. This would be like a new bride's expressing love to a picture of her husband and ignoring the man himself. It would be like having a son or daughter show great admiration and adoration for a picture of their mother and father and not showing love to their actual parents.

These things are "a shadow of things to come; but the body [the fulfillment] is of Christ" (Col. 2:17). Shadows don't last. Shadows are cast when light shines from behind some solid object. The false teachers thought that feast days, Sabbath days and the dietary laws were the reality. Actually they were only the shadows that pointed to the reality. All reality is in Jesus Christ. He is the truth. He is the Word. God has wrapped up in Jesus Christ all the reality that we will ever need. He has fulfilled the Law. Therefore, we are living in the light and not in the shadows. When we place ourselves under the

35

Law, not only are we putting ourselves under a yoke of bondage, not only are we making ourselves a child (cared for by a guardian), not only are we putting ourselves under a slave girl and a bond of indebtedness, but also we are putting ourselves back in the shadows.

The Law As a Mirror

In James 1 is a sixth picture of the Law: It is compared to *a mirror.* James 1:22-25 says, "But be ye doers of the word and not hearers only, deceiving your own selves. For if any be a hearer of the word, and not a doer, he is like a man beholding his natural face in a mirror; for he beholdeth himself, and goeth his way, and immediately forgetteth what manner of man he was. But whosoever looketh into the perfect law of liberty, and continueth in it, he being not a forgetful hearer but a doer of the work, this man shall be blessed in his deed." The Law is a mirror that reveals sin. You look into the mirror and see that your face is dirty, *but you don't wash your face in the mirror!* The mirror shows you that you are dirty, but the mirror cannot cleanse you. The Law is God's mirror to show us how dirty we are. When I read the Word of God, I realize that I am a sinner and therefore need a Saviour.

When you know Jesus Christ as your Saviour, the Word of God becomes your mirror, according to II Corinthians 3:18: "But we all, with unveiled face beholding as in a mirror the glory of the Lord, are changed into the same image from glory to glory, even as by the Spirit of the Lord." When the child of

God looks into the Word of God (the mirror) and sees the Son of God, he is transformed by the Spirit of God into the image of God for the glory of God. The Law never changed anybody; it is only a mirror that shows us our sin. When you have Jesus Christ as your Saviour and the Holy Spirit lives within you, the Word becomes a mirror that transforms you from glory to glory. You become more like the Lord Jesus Christ! If you put yourself under the Law, all you can do is look in the mirror and see how dirty you are. That creates guilt and condemnation, but it never changes you for the better. It always changes you for the worse.

The Law As a Husband

Our final picture of the Law is in Romans 7:1-4: It is compared to *a husband*. "Know ye not, brethren (for I speak to them that know the law), how that the law hath dominion over a man as long as he liveth? For the woman who hath an husband is bound by the law to her husband as long as he liveth; but if the husband be dead, she is loosed from the law of her husband. So, then if, while her husband liveth, she be married to another man, she shall be called an adulteress; but if her husband be dead, she is free from that law, so that she is no adulteress, though she be married to another man. Wherefore, my brethren, ye also are become dead to the law by the body of Christ, that ye should be married to another, even to him who is raised from the dead, that we should bring forth fruit unto God."

When a woman marries a man, she has a per-

manent, binding obligation. Israel was wedded to the Law. They had agreed to obey the Law. The Law was like a husband, giving directions to them and being in dominion over them. The interesting thing is this: Paul did not say that the husband died; he said that *we* died. The Law is not dead. The Law is very much alive. The Law is holy and just and good. We are the sinners. We are the ones who died. We have a new relationship to the Law because we have died. When Jesus died, we died with Him. When He arose, we arose with Him. Therefore, we are dead to the Law.

The Law is not dead to us. If you put yourself back under the Law, you will discover how powerful the Law is to condemn. But when you have been saved through Jesus Christ, you are united to Him in His death, burial and resurrection. This means you have died to the Law. You have been raised to walk in newness of life. You are married, not to the Law but to Jesus Christ. Your relationship is one of love and life, not one of Law.

Paul used marriage as an illustration of our relationship to the Law: "But now we are delivered from the law, that being dead in which we were held, that we should serve in newness of spirit and not in the oldness of the letter" (v. 6). Can you imagine a husband's putting up a list of rules and regulations in order to control his wife? No! How do a husband and wife build a happy home? Through a loving, living, growing relationship. You are married to Jesus Christ. You have His name. You share His wealth. One day you will live in His home. You enjoy

His love. You have His protection. You share His future. We are married to Jesus Christ. We are not married to the Law. We died to the Law. We have been delivered from the Law. Therefore, we can walk in newness of life and serve in newness of the Spirit because we don't have a relationship of obligation and galling responsibility. We have a loving, living relationship to a wonderful Saviour, and He is our husband.

How wonderful it is to be united to Jesus Christ in life and in love but not in Law. We obey Him, not because we fear Him but because we love Him. We obey Him, not because He holds threats over our heads but because He blesses us.

To review these seven pictures: We are no longer under the yoke of the Law, controlled by guardians, related to slave girls, owing a bond of indebtedness. We are not in the shadows. We are not looking in a mirror that makes us look dirty. We are not married to a domineering husband. No, we have a wonderful, living relationship with the Lord Jesus Christ! We are free from the Law, free to live for Him.

Chapter 5

Freedom From Sin

Every Christian has to battle with three enemies: the world, the flesh and the Devil. These three enemies come from our old life. In Ephesians 2:1-3 Paul described our old life: "And you hath he made alive, who were dead in trespasses and sins; in which in times past ye walked according to the course of this world [there is the world], according to the prince of the power of the air, the spirit that now worketh in the sons of disobedience [there is the Devil]; among whom also we all had our manner of life in times past in the lusts of our flesh [there is the flesh]."

Before I was a Christian, I lived according to the dictates of this world. I was controlled by the power of Satan, and I lived to satisfy the desires of the flesh. When I became a Christian, I was set free from these enemies, but they are still enemies! They still want to attack me and defeat me. You and I face a struggle to overcome these enemies. It's wonderful to know that Jesus Christ has made provision for us to have victory. Through Jesus Christ, we can have freedom from the sins of the flesh. This is not to say that we can live perfectly sinless lives,

because "if we say that we have no sin, we deceive ourselves, and the truth is not in us" (I John 1:8). But it is possible for us to live in victory over deliberate sin if we will simply follow the instructions that God gives to us in Romans 6.

The theme of Romans 6 is how to stop doing bad things, how to live in victory over the flesh. In this chapter Paul gave three very simple instructions: know, reckon and yield. In the first ten verses he talked about what we should *know*. Then in verse 11 he said we should *reckon* on what we know, and in verses 12-23 he told us we should *yield*. He gave instruction to the mind: *know*. Then he gave instruction to the heart: *reckon*. Finally, he gave instruction to the will: *yield*.

What We Should Know

In the first three chapters of Romans, Paul dealt with sin and concluded that the whole world stands condemned before God. What, then, is the answer? The answer is salvation through faith in Jesus Christ, and this he discussed in Romans 4 and 5. In chapter 4 he referred to Abraham and showed that Abraham was saved the same way everybody else has to be saved—by faith. In chapter 5 he went all the way back to Adam and pointed out that we are in the mess we are in because of Adam's fall. In Adam we all fell; in Christ we can be made alive again.

At this point somebody might raise some objections. (There are always those who raise objec-

tions!) Paul said, "But where sin abounded, grace did much more abound" (v. 20). "If we are saved by grace through faith apart from works," says the objector, "why don't we just continue in sin that grace may abound? The more we sin, the more God's grace may abound, and the more God will be glorified!"

I often hear from people who do not believe in the doctrine of "the perseverance of the saints"; that is, that once you are saved, you are saved forever. They write to me and say, "Brother Wiersbe, if you tell people they are saved forever, they'll go out and sin!" This is the objection that Paul dealt with in Romans 6. He said that we need to know three fundamental truths. We need to know something about sin, something about the work of Christ on the cross and something about ourselves.

About Sin

We need to know something about sin. What did Paul say about sin in this chapter? He said that *sin enslaves.* Sin always begins with freedom, but it leads to slavery. You may be playing with sin right now, or you may be contemplating sin. You are a believer in Jesus Christ, but perhaps ideas of sin are lingering in the back of your mind. I want to warn you that sin enters as a *guest;* then sin becomes a *friend*—you get to know each other and like each other. Then sin becomes a *servant.* It promises to serve you and to give you pleasure. But that servant becomes a *master,* that master becomes a *tyrant,* and that tyrant becomes a *destroyer.* Sin always

begins with freedom and ends with destruction and slavery.

"For we ourselves also were once foolish, disobedient, deceived, serving various lusts and pleasures, living in malice and envy, hateful, and hating one another" (Titus 3:3). That's the way it was before we were born again. People have the idea that sin is serving them, but they are wrong. They are serving sin! Paul told us very clearly that Christians are "freed from sin" (Rom. 6:7) and "should not serve sin" (v. 6). You and I need to deal drastically with sin. That's the first thing Paul wanted us to know. He wanted us to know that sin is a terrible tyrant that will dominate our life, if we permit it.

About Christ's Work

Second, *he wanted us to know something about Christ's work on the cross.* "How shall we, that are dead to sin, live any longer in it? Know ye not that, as many of us as were baptized into Jesus Christ were baptized into his death? Therefore, we are buried with him by baptism into death, that as Christ was raised up from the dead by the glory of the Father, even so we also should walk in newness of life. For if we have been planted together in the likeness of his death, we shall be also in the likeness of his resurrection; knowing this, that our old man is crucified with him, that the body of sin might be destroyed, that henceforth we should not serve sin. For he that is dead is freed from sin. Now if we be dead with Christ, we believe that we shall also live with him, knowing that Christ, being raised from the

43

dead, dieth no more; death hath no more dominion over him. For in that he died, he died unto sin once; but in that he liveth, he liveth unto God" (Rom. 6:2-10).

There is a contrast in emphasis between Romans 5 and Romans 6. In Romans 5 Paul dealt with *substitution*—Christ died for me. But in Romans 6 he dealt with *identification*—I died with Him. In Romans 5 Paul said that Jesus died *for* sin, but in Romans 6 he said that Jesus died *unto* sin. What's the difference? According to chapter 5 Jesus Christ died to deal with the *penalty* of sin, but according to chapter 6 Jesus Christ died to break the *power* of sin. Chapter 5 deals with justification, our standing before God. Chapter 6 deals with sanctification, our victory through the Lord Jesus Christ. We have an entirely new relationship with sin because of the work of the Lord Jesus Christ.

When you trusted Jesus Christ as your Saviour, the Holy Spirit of God baptized you into the Body of Christ. This baptism did not occur after conversion but was simultaneous with conversion (I Cor. 12:13). Every believer has the gift of the Holy Spirit, and every believer has been identified with Jesus Christ in His death, burial, resurrection and ascension. This is the beautiful truth of Romans 6. This is why Paul said, "What shall we say then? Shall we continue in sin, that grace may abound? God forbid" (vv. 1,2). After all we have experienced in Jesus Christ, how can we continue in sin?

To begin with, we are *dead to sin* (v. 2). According to Romans 6:7, the old man is crucified: "For he

that is dead is freed from sin." Sin is not dead to me, but *I am dead to sin.* Sin is very much alive, but we are dead to sin because we have been buried with Christ and raised up to newness of life. We have been crucified with Christ.

We have been freed from sin. "Being, then, made free from sin, ye became the servants of righteousness" (v. 18). "But now being made free from sin, and become servants to God, ye have your fruit unto holiness, and the end everlasting life" (v. 22).

Please understand your new position in Jesus Christ. When Jesus died, you died in Him and with Him. When He was buried, your old life was buried in Him and with Him. When He arose, you arose with Him in newness of life. You are in Jesus Christ, and you have a new relationship to sin. You are dead to sin. The old man has been crucified. You are freed from sin, and therefore, you have the privilege of living in victory over sin.

About Yourself

Third, *you need to know something about yourself.* You must choose your master. A famous British preacher, Dr. P. T. Forsyth, used to say that our purpose in life is not to find our freedom but to find our master. When you find the right master, then you will have the right kind of freedom. If sin is your master, then you will serve sin and have a life of defeat, despair, disappointment and emptiness. But if Jesus Christ is your Master, then you will have a life of victory, a life of vitality. You can walk in

newness of life, in a marvelous life of joy and victory. You have to choose your master.

What We Should Reckon

He went on to say in Romans 6:11, "Likewise, reckon ye also yourselves to be dead indeed unto sin, but alive unto God through Jesus Christ, our Lord." Nineteen times in the Book of Romans he used the word (*logizomai*) that is translated "reckoned." Sometimes it is translated "impute" or "count." This is the second instruction that he gives: *reckon*.

What does it mean to reckon? To reckon means to rely on, to claim for yourself that which God says is true in the Bible. Suppose that I owed you $25 and that I wrote you a check and mailed it to you. You say, "My, but this is a beautiful check! What a lovely picture on the check!" You put the check in your pocket, and you never cash it. You are not reckoning. But when you go to the bank and endorse the check, you are reckoning. You are saying, "I believe that what Wiersbe has said on this check is true. I believe there is money in the bank; therefore, I am going to cash the check."

How do you know that you died with Jesus Christ on the cross? The Bible says you did. If I were to ask you, "How many crosses were on Calvary?" you would say, "Three." Jesus was in the middle, and two thieves were on either side. How do you know this? How do you know that there were two thieves with Jesus on Calvary? Because the Bible says so. Well, the same Bible that says two thieves died with

46

Jesus *also says that you died with Jesus!* If you really believe the one, you have to believe the other. To reckon simply means to believe that what the Word says is true—true in *my* life.

Reckoning is not trying to work up an experience. I find saints who are always trying to work up an experience. Reckoning is simply believing that what God said in Romans 6 is true. Sin is not dead to me, but I am dead to sin. I am not trying to work up an emotional experience. I am simply believing what God said. That's reckoning. Reckoning simply means that I am acting in faith. I am united with Jesus Christ. God's Word is true. The work of Christ is completed. Therefore, what God says in the Word is true in my life.

Are you reckoning yourself to be dead indeed unto sin (that's the negative) but alive unto God through Jesus Christ our Lord (that's the positive)? The key word here is the word "Lord." Jesus Christ is not just our Saviour, but He is also our Lord. Are you reckoning on this?

Let me review what we have studied. The first instruction Paul gave in Romans 6 is *know*. We should know something about sin (it enslaves us), about the work of Christ (He has freed us), about ourselves (we must choose our master). His second instruction was *reckon*. This is the work of the heart, believing for myself that what God says in the Word is true in my life.

Chapter 6

Freedom From Sin (cont.)

Paul gave believers three instructions in Romans 6—know, reckon and yield. If we follow these instructions, we will have victory over the flesh.

What We Should Yield

Paul's third instruction in Romans 6 was *yield.* "Let not sin, therefore, reign in your mortal body, that ye should obey it in its lusts" (v. 12). A distinction is made between *sin* and *the body.* Once in a while I receive mail from radio listeners asking whether or not the body is sinful. No, the body is not sinful. The body is neutral. But a force at work within the body (which the Bible calls the flesh, the old man) wants us to use our body in a sinful way. In verse 12 of Romans 6, Paul began with a word addressed to my will: "Let not." My mind must *know* the truth, my heart must *reckon* on this truth, but my will must *act* on this truth. "Let not sin, therefore, reign in your mortal body, that ye should obey it in its lusts."

Sin comes in as a guest and then becomes a friend. Then the friend becomes a servant, and the servant becomes a master. You think you are con-

trolling sin, but sin is controlling you. "Neither yield ye your members [the parts of your body] as instruments of unrighteousness unto sin" (v. 13). The Greek word translated "instruments" means weapons. It also can be applied to tools. My hands, my feet, my tongue—the various parts of my body—can be used by sin to do unrighteousness, or they can be used by God to do righteousness. The body itself is neutral. *The master* makes the difference. If sin is your master, then you will live in unrighteousness. If Christ is your Master, then you will live in holiness. "But yield yourselves unto God, as those that are alive from the dead, and your members as instruments of righteousness unto God" (v. 13).

Paul was talking about a living sacrifice, one who is "alive from the dead." Our Lord Jesus Christ is in heaven today with a glorified body. He is a living sacrifice, for He bears the marks of Calvary on that glorified body. The only works of man in heaven today that I know of are the wounds on the body of the Lord Jesus. Jesus is a living sacrifice. In the Old Testament Isaac was a living sacrifice. Isaac yielded himself to his father and willingly put himself on the altar. He was bound and, to all intents and purposes, was slain. God stopped Abraham from killing his son. But as far as God was concerned, Isaac died and was (in a type) raised from the dead. Isaac was freed and became a living sacrifice.

Paul applied this same truth in Romans 12:1,2. These verses are so familiar that sometimes we overlook them or take them for granted. The Greek

49

word translated "yield" in Romans 6 (*paristemi*) is the same word translated "present" in Romans 12:1. "I beseech you therefore, brethren, by the mercies of God, that ye present your bodies a living sacrifice, holy, acceptable unto God, which is your reasonable service."

Our Bodies

God wants you to give Him your body. That sounds very ordinary, but it's one of the most spiritual things you can do! If God is going to use you, He must have your body. When Jesus Christ came to earth to redeem us, He had to have a body. In order to get His message of salvation to a wicked world, Jesus Christ must have a Body—the Church. God can use my fingers to write letters. He can use my feet to make visits in homes. He can use my lips to speak the message of truth. That's why you should take good care of your body—it's the only tool you've got. A person would be a fool to pour sand into his gas tank, wouldn't he? He would wreck the car. Well, people do some foolish things with their bodies. God wants your body as a holy sacrifice, as a complete sacrifice to Him. Just as Jesus gave His body on the cross for you, God wants you to give your body on the altar for Him.

Our Minds

Paul went on to say in Romans 12:2, "But be ye transformed by the renewing of your mind." Not only should I give God my body, but *I should also give Him my mind.* Why? Because my mind con-

trols my body. What you think about is what you do. You say, "Well, I've thought about things I've never done." If you keep thinking about them long enough, you'll do them! "As he thinketh in his heart, so he is," says Proverbs 23:7. "Be not conformed to this world" (Rom. 12:2). Don't think the way the world thinks. "Blessed is the man who walketh not in the counsel of the ungodly, nor standeth in the way of sinners, nor sitteth in the seat of the scornful" (Ps. 1:1).

Our Wills

"Be not conformed to this world, but be ye transformed by the renewing of your mind, that ye may prove what is that good, and acceptable, and perfect, will of God" (Rom. 12:2). *God also wants my will.* God wants you to yield your body, your mind and your will to Him. He wants you to do this because you love Him. He wants your heart. Because of all that God has done for you, you should gladly yield yourself to Him.

Results of Yielding

When we yield ourselves to God, a wonderful thing happens: *We get victory over sin!* "For sin shall not have dominion over you; for ye are not under the law but under grace" (Rom. 6:14). What does the Law have to do with victory? According to I Corinthians 15:56, "The strength of sin is the law." Romans 7 teaches us that the very law that tells me what I should not do arouses in me the desire to do it. The Law is good, but I am sinful. The Law never

51

changed a person's nature. The Law cannot control sin, and it cannot change sinners. What does the Law do? It reveals sin. "The strength of sin is the law." The minute you say to a child, "Don't do that!" he starts figuring out some way to do it. Why? Because he has a nature within that does not want to obey the law. "What then? Shall we sin, because we are not under the law, but under grace? God forbid" (6:15).

You and I must yield ourselves to God. Then He becomes the master of our lives. We give him our body, our mind, our will, our heart. We allow the Word of God to transform our minds, and as He transforms our minds by His Word, He guides us by His Spirit, and we become the servants of God. It is a beautiful thing to be set free from this old life and to walk in what the Bible calls "newness of life." "But God be thanked, that whereas ye were the servants of sin, ye have obeyed from the heart that form of doctrine which was delivered you. Being, then, made free from sin, ye became the servants of righteousness" (vv. 17,18).

Paul applied this in verses 19 and 20: "I speak after the manner of men [I'm using a human illustration] because of the infirmity of your flesh; for as ye have yielded your members servants to uncleanness and to iniquity, unto iniquity [when you were lost, you yielded the parts of your body to sin]; even so now yield your members servants to righteousness, unto holiness. For when ye were the servants of sin, ye were free from righteousness." That's a terrible freedom, isn't it? We were in the bondage of

sin, and we couldn't perform righteous deeds. Now we are in Jesus Christ, righteous in Him; therefore, we can be free from sin.

Paul asked an important question in verse 21: "What fruit had ye then in those things of which ye are now ashamed?" Think about that. Have you ever said, "I would like to go back to my old life"? I hope not! What was the blessing of your old life? Have you forgotten what it was like to be in bondage to sin? The next time you're tempted to go back into the world or to serve the flesh, just remember what you were before. In Deuteronomy God told the Jews to remind themselves regularly that they were once in bondage in Egypt. The trouble was that when the Israelites thought about Egypt, they thought only about the leeks and the onions and the garlic. They remembered the good things. They forgot their taskmasters, their chains and their bondage. "What fruit had ye then in those things of which ye are now ashamed? For the end of those things is death. But now being made free from sin, and become servants to God [yielding yourself to God], ye have your fruit unto holiness, and the end everlasting life" (Rom. 6:21,22). What a marvelous thing—to produce fruit unto holiness, to have a fruitful life! Now that we are in Jesus Christ and yielded to Him, we can produce fruit!

"For the wages of sin is death" (v. 23). Paul didn't write this verse to unbelievers in a rescue mission. He wrote Romans 6:23 to believers in a local assembly. Samson discovered the wages of sin. When a Christian plays around with sin, sin

53

becomes his master, then sin becomes his tyrant, and then sin becomes his destroyer. King Saul discovered that. There were Christians in Corinth who had sinned, and God had to take their lives. "There is a sin unto death," we're told in I John 5:16. If you work for sin, you'll receive the wages that sin pays, and the wages of sin is death. But if you are working for God, if you have yielded yourself to God, "the gift of God is eternal life through Jesus Christ, our Lord" (Rom. 6:23). Take your choice.

Know. Know what? Know that sin enslaves. Know that Jesus Christ has set you free from this slavery and that you must choose your master.

Reckon. Reckon that what God says in His Word is true. Believe it for yourself.

Yield. Present your body, your mind, your will, your heart to God. Let the Holy Spirit work in your life to overcome the flesh and to produce fruit unto God. This means a daily yielding. It sometimes means a struggle against sin. We are not talking about some once-for-all decision that puts you on such a high plane that you will never again be tempted. You may have some occasional falls. Then you get up and say, "Lord, I'm sorry, forgive me." He forgives you, and you get going again.

"The victorious Christian life," said Alexander Whyte, "is a series of new beginnings." As you spend time in the Word of God and prayer, as you fellowship with other Christians, you find yourself growing in your Christian freedom. When Jesus died for you, He died not only to rescue you from the *penalty* of sin, which is eternal death, but He

54

died to rescue you from the very *power* of sin. My prayer is that all of us might experience this beautiful life of fruitfulness and freedom to the glory of God. The Lord Jesus Christ did not die to make me a slave. He died to make me a son.

I would urge you to meditate on Romans 6 and to notice these three simple instructions: *know, reckon, yield.* Then yield yourself daily to the Lord. Your freedom in Christ will make you free from sin, and you will have victory over the Tempter to the glory of God.

Chapter 7

Freedom From Men

It is dangerous when spiritual leaders become dictators and we become enslaved to people. "Not that we have dominion over your faith," wrote the Apostle Paul, "but are helpers of your joy" (II Cor. 1:24). In I Corinthians 7:17-24 Paul laid down a basic principle that we should not be subject to people.

"But as God hath distributed to every man, as the Lord hath called every one, so let him walk. And so ordain I in all churches. Is any man called being circumcised? Let him not become uncircumcised. Is any called in uncircumcision? Let him not be circumcised. Circumcision is nothing, and uncircumcision is nothing, but the keeping of the commandments of God. Let every man abide in the same calling in which he was called. Art thou called, being a servant? Care not for it; but if thou mayest be made free, use it rather. For he that is called in the Lord, being a servant, is the Lord's freeman; likewise also he that is called, being free, is Christ's servant. Ye are bought with a price; be not ye the servants of men. Brethren, let every man, in whatever state he is called, there abide with God" (I Cor. 7:17-24).

Let's consider this subject of freedom from people from three different aspects.

The Setting

First of all, consider *the setting.* If we don't understand the setting of this passage, we are going to make some false interpretations. Paul was having problems with the Corinthians because of their abuse of their new freedom. The Corinthian church was comprised of people some of whom had lived in gross sin. Many of them had been involved in very wicked practices, and now they had freedom in the Lord Jesus Christ.

Galatians 3:28 is the key that will help us in studying this chapter: "There is neither Jew nor Greek, there is neither bond nor free, there is neither male nor female; for ye are all one in Christ Jesus." The Corinthian believers knew that truth, but they were taking it to the extreme. They were making use of their freedom to the point of license.

For example, they said, "When you are saved and in Jesus Christ, there is neither male nor female; so that abolishes our marriages." In I Corinthians 7:1-16 Paul explained the Christian marriage relationship. When a person becomes a Christian, it does not abolish his marriage relationship. Rather it gives new potential for victory and blessing in that marriage relationship. The women in the Corinthian church were carrying their freedom a little bit too far, but so were the men.

"There is neither Jew nor Greek" (Gal. 3:28).

Paul dealt with this in I Corinthians 7:17-20. The Jews who got saved wanted to become like the Gentiles and tried to erase the mark of the covenant from their body. On the other hand, the Gentiles wanted to become like the Jews! There is neither Jew nor Gentile in Jesus Christ, but this does not erase one's nationality. When I was saved, my nationality did not change.

"There is neither bond nor free" (Gal. 3:28). He dealt with this in I Corinthians 7:21-24. Some slaves who had been saved said, "We are no longer slaves! We don't have to obey our masters anymore!" Paul wrote to them and said, "You had better be careful how you use your freedom." They were tempted to make changes that God never meant to be made. He did tell the slaves that if an opportunity came along for freedom, they should use it. But they were to use it for the glory of God, not for their own selfish purposes.

In Jesus Christ "there is neither male nor female" (Gal. 3:28); but when you were saved, your sex did not change. In Jesus Christ there is neither Jew nor Gentile; but when you were saved, your racial or national origins did not change. In Jesus Christ there is neither bond nor free; but when you were saved, your economic or social status did not change. Salvation gives us the potential to make the most out of every situation. Salvation is a *spiritual* change. It can bring about changes in the home, on the job and in society. But God doesn't work from the outside in; He works from the inside out. Paul was very careful to tell those people that their free-

dom in Jesus Christ must not be abused and turned into license.

The Meaning

Let's look now at *the meaning* of the passage. Paul laid down a fundamental principle here that he gave in all churches; namely, *remain as you are, and let God make the changes.*

"But as God hath distributed to every man, as the Lord hath called every one, so let him walk. . . . Let every man abide in the same calling in which he was called. . . . Brethren, let every man, in whatever state he is called, there abide with God" (I Cor. 7:17,20,24). Remain as you are. Don't try to make a lot of radical changes immediately. Allow the changes to come from within. Paul reminded us that we are free, but we are not independent. No Christian can be independent of other Christians. *But no Christian must be dependent on others.* That is, no pastor should be a spiritual dictator in the lives of his people. No Sunday school teacher should be a spiritual dictator in the lives of his class members. Jesus warned us not to call any person on earth our spiritual father (see Matt. 23:8-12). There is a sense in which those who lead us to Christ are our spiritual fathers (I Cor. 4:15), but not in the sense of being dictators over our lives. The slaves were to consider themselves free in Christ, but they were still slaves. The masters were to consider themselves Christ's slaves, but they were still masters. You are free from the domination of people, but this does not make you independent. This should not

59

cause you to make all sorts of radical changes. Allow the changes to come from within.

We Are Called by God

Paul presented four arguments to prove that we should remain as we are and let God make the changes from within. First, *we are called by God.* "As the Lord hath called every one" (I Cor. 7:17). This idea is repeated in verses 18,20,21,22 and 24. In fact, he used the words "called" and "calling" nine times in this passage. He concluded the passage: "Brethren, let every man, in whatever state he is called, there abide with God" (v. 24). This does not mean that if you are offered a promotion on your job, you should turn it down. He was saying that, because you are a Christian, you don't try to make a lot of radical changes. Let God do the changing. You have been called by God.

We Have Been Assigned by God

First Corinthians 7:17 says, "As God hath distributed to every man." The word "distributed" means "assigned to him." Our place in society, our job, our gifts are assignments from God. This is Paul's second argument. You have been called by God, and *you have been assigned by God.* Some slave may say, "I can't see how being a slave is a gift from God!" That is not for us to argue or debate. God knows what he is doing, and when God wants to make the changes, they will be made. We should not run around trying to make all sorts of radical changes just because we are Christians. That does

not mean we should not try to better our condition. Nobody wants to remain in a difficult situation. But if this is the place that God assigned, we have to accept it as His will until He changes it. However, as Paul said to the slaves, if the opportunity for improvement comes, make use of it. But be sure the changes come from God.

We Belong to God

The third argument is given in I Corinthians 7:23: "Ye are bought with a price; be not ye the servants of men." *You belong to God.* The value of an object is measured by the price you pay for it. It's amazing what some people will pay for certain objects. Jesus Christ shed His blood for us! That shows how valuable we are to God. "Ye are bought with a price." You belong to God, He purchased you. Therefore, "be not ye the servants of men." The servant serves the one who purchased him. We have been purchased by Jesus Christ; so we must serve Him.

We Should Abide With God

In I Corinthians 7:24 Paul gave a fourth argument: "Let every man . . . abide with God." *We are to abide with God.* If you are where God has placed you, doing the job God has given you to do, you are abiding with God. If you rebel against God's will, you will not abide with God. If we don't abide with God, we cannot bear spiritual fruit. And so his argument is simply this: Remain as you are. Let God make the changes because He assigns us our ministry in life.

The Application

The third aspect of freedom from men is *living it*. How can you and I practically apply this truth in our lives?

I fear that many people are under bondage to others. They live in fear of other people. Proverbs 29:25 says that the fear of men brings a snare. We must not be independent of people. We must never say, "I don't care how they feel or what they think." We *must* care, but we must not be subservient. We must not be enslaved to the opinions of others.

I face this problem week in and week out. People phone or write and want me to come to their church or their conference to speak. Most of the time I have to say no. I simply don't have time to be every place and still do my work as I should. They tell me that the Lord has led them to invite me. But it's strange the Lord would lead six different people to invite me for the same day! The Lord knows I can't be in six places at the same time.

If I were afraid of people and wanted simply to please people, I would find myself in the hospital. We must be very careful not to serve people but to serve God. If we are serving God as we should, we will find ourselves serving people too. There is always time to do the will of God. Paul said, "Ourselves your servants for Jesus' sake" (II Cor. 4:5). He didn't say, "Ourselves your servants for *our* sake or for *your* sake." But he said, "For Jesus' sake."

Let me say a word to church members. Your

62

pastor is not your slave. You say, "Well, if he doesn't do what I want him to do, I'll quit going to church." That's a pretty immature attitude to have. Your pastor is not there to be a slave to all the people. He is the servant of God. He may have to say no to you at times. When I was a pastor, folks would invite us over for meals or to one activity or another, and I would often have to say, "I'm sorry, we cannot come." Sometimes people would get disturbed. But I had work to do. I had meditating, praying and writing to do. I had to live by my priorities.

We should not have to be enslaved to *the commandments of men*. In Matthew 15:9 the Lord Jesus warned us not to listen to the doctrines of men—the commandments of men. There is so much tradition these days! Churches have man-made traditions that cannot be backed up by the Word of God.

In John 5:41-44 Jesus warned about *the praise of men*. "I receive not honor from men. But I know you, that ye have not the love of God in you. . . . How can ye believe, who receive honor one of another, and seek not the honor that cometh from God only?" Beware of the praise of others. I fear that Christian workers often desire to please people and receive their praise and perhaps get a degree from some school or be used in an important meeting. This is dangerous.

In Galatians 1:10-12 Paul warned about *the authority of men*. My pastor has authority over me, and the government has authority over me. But

Paul warned us not to allow people to dictate what our ministry should be and not to try to please people in our ministry. "For do I now seek the favor of men, or of God? Or do I seek to please men? For if I yet pleased men, I should not be the servant of Christ" (Gal. 1:10). That is a pretty plain statement! Some people bow down to please other people, bow to their authority; and by doing so, they are not serving God.

Beware of *the wisdom of men* (I Cor. 2:5). Be sure you follow the wisdom of God. And beware of *the fear of men.* In Matthew 10:24-28, Jesus explained that all people can do is kill your body, but God can destroy both body and soul in hell!

Don't bow down to human commandments and traditions. Don't live for the praise of other people. Don't live under the dictatorial authority of people. Be careful that people are not running your life or your ministry. Watch out for the wisdom of people. Don't fear people. In other words, "Ye are bought with a price; be not ye the servants of men" (I Cor. 7:23).

It is wonderful to discover this freedom from people, to not worry about whether they like you or dislike you, whether they approve or disapprove of your ministry. If you are doing the will of God, according to the Word of God, in the power of the Spirit of God, for the glory of God, then you are the servant of God. "Ye are bought with a price; be not ye the servants of men" (v. 23).

You may say, "I have never murdered anybody." I'm glad for that, but Jesus said that if you hate someone in your heart, you have committed murder in your heart. We may say, "Well, I have never bowed down before an idol." That may be true, but is Jesus Christ *first* in your life? Are there other gods demanding your allegiance and your obedience? What are you sacrificing to today? It is possible for us to outwardly conform to the standards of the Law but inwardly be committing all kinds of sin. The Law is not only *against* us, but the Law is *contrary* to us.

The Law itself is "holy, and just, and good" (Rom. 7:12). Nowhere does the Bible say that the Law is bad. *We* are the ones who are bad. If that which is holy and just and good shows us how bad we are, then we really must be bad! God does not have to use *bad* things to show us how bad we are. He uses *good* things—such as the Law—to show us how bad we are! This shows us the extent of the depravity of the human heart!

So you and I had a bond of indebtedness that we could not pay. We were totally bankrupt. The Lord Jesus told a parable about two men (see Luke 7:40-50). One owed 500 denarii and the other owed 50 denarii. (One denarius equalled a day's wages.) Neither could pay, but the banker graciously forgave both of them! You and I were completely bankrupt before God. Sinners may not think they are bankrupt. They may think they are rich. But in the sight of God, we are poor and wretched and blind and naked. We have nothing in ourselves. Our

32

Chapter 8

Freedom From the Past

We cannot change the past, but we can be changed by the past. Many people are controlled by past sins, past regrets and past failures. The past should be a rudder to guide us and not an anchor to drag us back. In I Timothy 1:12-17 Paul talked about his relationship to his past.

"And I thank Christ Jesus, our Lord, who hath enabled me, in that he counted me faithful, putting me into the ministry, who was before a blasphemer, and a persecutor, and injurious; but I obtained mercy, because I did it ignorantly in unbelief. And the grace of our Lord was exceedingly abundant with faith and love which is in Christ Jesus. This is a faithful saying, and worthy of all acceptance, that Christ Jesus came into the world to save sinners, of whom I am chief. Nevertheless, for this cause I obtained mercy, that in me first Jesus Christ might show forth all long-suffering, for a pattern to them who should hereafter believe on him to life everlasting. Now unto the King eternal, immortal, invisible, the only wise God, be honor and glory forever and ever. Amen."

Paul was able to look at his past and, in spite of his

failures, praise God. Paul was not shackled by past failures, past sins or past mistakes. You and I need to learn how to be free from our past. Someone has said that most of the people in the world are being crucified between two thieves—the fear of tomorrow and the regrets of yesterday. How many people carry a heavy burden of past regret and past failure! Though you cannot change the past, you are being changed by the past. How can we be freed from the tyranny of the past? I would suggest, on the basis of Scripture, that we need to take some definite steps.

Accept God's Forgiveness

We must accept God's forgiveness.

Paul said, "This is a faithful saying, and worthy of all acceptance, that Christ Jesus came into the world to save sinners, of whom I am chief" (I Tim. 1:15). Paul had no illusions about himself. He knew that what he had done was wrong. He had been a blasphemer, and he had caused other people to blaspheme. He had said, "Jesus Christ is an impostor! He is not the Messiah!" He forced other people to make this confession. Paul was a persecutor. He was injurious, or proud and insolent. A modern equivalent would be our word "bully."

And yet Paul obtained mercy! He mentioned mercy in verse 13 and again in verse 16. "Nevertheless, for this cause I obtained mercy" (v. 16). In verse 14 he talked about "the grace of our Lord." He also mentioned *faith* and *love* in Christ Jesus. In other words, Paul eventually accepted God's forgiveness. He confessed that he was a sinner. He admitted that he had done wrong. He rested upon the grace and the mercy of God. He experienced the love of God and the abundance of the grace of God. God changed him!

If you are a Christian, God has completely dealt with all of your sin—not just *part* of your sin but *all* of your sin. You are justified. That means God has declared you righteous in Jesus Christ, and that will never change. "Therefore, being justified by faith, we have peace with God" (Rom. 5:1). We can look at our past and know it's been taken care of. We can look at our present and know that God is with us. We can look at the future and know that God is going before us.

We have been regenerated. What does that mean? It means we have been born again. We have a new nature within us, and that new nature enables us to live a new life. We have been redeemed. We have been purchased out of the slavery of sin and set free to serve Jesus Christ. We are no longer slaves of sin, which means we are no longer slaves of the past. We have been forgiven—completely, totally, graciously—on the basis of Calvary. "In whom we have redemption through his blood, even the forgiveness of sins. . . . And you, being dead in your sins and the uncircumcision of your flesh, hath he made alive together with him, having forgiven you all trespasses" (Col. 1:14; 2:13).

I think it was Dr. Ironside who had this experience. He had been preaching on the fact that when you trust Jesus as your Saviour, *all* of your sins are forgiven—past, present and future. Someone approached him afterward and said, "I believe that when I was saved, Jesus took care of my *past* sins but not my future sins." Dr. Ironside quietly asked, "And how many of your sins were past when Jesus died?" That solves the problem, doesn't it?

Don't allow the fact that you used to be a wicked person before you trusted Jesus to cripple your life and ministry today. You are a new person in Jesus Christ. You still have all the potential for sin, but you have experienced the grace of God, the love of God, the mercy of God. Paul called himself the chief of sinners, and yet he accepted God's forgiveness. He believed in Jesus Christ, and this freed him from his past. We need to accept God's forgiveness.

An interesting story in Genesis 50 relates to Joseph and his brothers. You know, of course, that Joseph's brothers lied about him and sold him as a slave. Then Joseph became the second in command in Egypt. Joseph had the power and authority to prosecute his brothers if he had wanted to; instead, he wept and forgave them. But they had a difficult time accepting his forgiveness! When their father, Jacob, died, the brothers were sure that Joseph would really "take it out on them." So they sent a messenger to Joseph and said, "Our father told us to be sure to tell you to forgive us." Joseph wept and said, in effect, "Don't you believe me? I've already told you that I have forgiven you!"

Don't be shackled by the past. Live for the present. That is step one: Accept God's forgiveness.

Forgive Others

Forgive others. One evidence of true repentance is that we can forgive others. "If ye forgive men their trespasses, your heavenly Father will also forgive you; but if ye forgive not men their trespasses, neither will your Father forgive your trespasses" (Matt. 6:14,15). Our Lord was not saying that we have to *earn* forgiveness. He was saying that we have to give evidence of a broken heart. If I want to receive God's forgiveness, I have to repent of my sin and turn my back on it—and that includes an unforgiving spirit toward others.

In Matthew 18 the Lord Jesus told His disciples to forgive one another. Peter asked, "Well, if my brother sins against me, how many times should I forgive him? Seven times?" (see v. 21).

Jesus said, "No, 70 times 7" (v. 22). That's 490 times! Obviously, my brother is not going to repeat the same sin 490 times. *But I may remember his sin 490 times!* I think our Lord was saying, "Every time you think about what your brother did to you, forgive him." Then He told the parable about the king who audited his books and discovered that one of his servants was robbing him of a large amount of money. So the king was going to sell the man and all that he had to pay the debt. But the man fell before the king and begged for forgiveness, and the king forgave him. But the servant went out of the king's presence and found a fellow servant who owed him just a few dollars. He grabbed the man, shook him and said, "Pay me what you owe me!" The man

69

begged for forgiveness, but the servant ignored his request and threw the man in prison.

This servant was forgiven a huge debt, but he would not forgive his fellow servant a very small debt. That unforgiving servant was handed over to tormentors to be punished until he paid his debt. Sometimes God's people carry with them the shackles of the past because they have an unforgiving spirit. "And be ye kind one to another, tenderhearted, forgiving one another, even as God, for Christ's sake, hath forgiven you" (Eph. 4:32).

William Sangster was a great Methodist preacher in Great Britain. One Christmas he was making out his Christmas card list. His wife looked at the list and said, "Surely you're not going to send a card to *him*," naming the person. Sangster asked, "Why not?" His wife asked, "Do you remember what he did to you and what he said about you?" Sangster thought for a moment and said, "Oh yes, yes, now I do remember—but I had made it a point to remember to forget."

All of us need to remember to forget. We must learn to forgive others. That's step two.

Forgive Yourself

Forgive yourself.

Many people cannot forgive themselves. Do you know why? Because they are proud. They say, "I told a lie, and I can't forgive myself!" Abraham lied about his wife. They say, "I lost my temper, and I was so angry!" Moses lost his temper one day and

70

killed a man. He also lost his temper and disobeyed God by striking the rock. They say, "I've had such impure thoughts! How could I do that?" David had impure thoughts and committed some impure deeds. They say, "I denied the Lord! I could have stood up and witnessed, but I didn't!" Peter denied the Lord three times.

Are you better than any of these men? Pride makes me say, "Oh, how could I have done that?" But humility ought to make me say, "I'm surprised I don't do worse." You can't drive these thoughts out of your mind. You say, "I wish I could forget what I said to her." "I wish I could forget what I did to him," but you cannot. If you bury these thoughts in your personality, they will just create problems.

What should you do? *When you remember these thoughts, turn them into prayer and praise.* When you remember the things you have done, forgive yourself, and you will end up doing what Paul did— praising God: "Now unto the King eternal, immortal, invisible, the only wise God, be honor and glory forever and ever" (I Tim. 1:17). God was able to use Paul as a pattern and as encouragement to others.

Forgive yourself. Don't hold grudges against yourself. Turn your memories of sin into praise and prayer. Trust God to bring something good out of it. You may not see how any good can come out of what you did, so leave it to God.

I have often reminded people that David committed two great sins: he committed adultery with Bathsheba (a sin of the flesh), and he numbered the people and took a census (a sin of the spirit). Seventy thousand people died because David numbered the people.

But the interesting thing is what God did with all this. David married Bathsheba, and Solomon was born. When David confessed his sin of numbering the people, he built an altar on a piece of property he had bought, and on that piece of property *Solomon built the temple.* Only God can take a man's two greatest sins and build a temple out of it.

You may have done some things that were wrong. You suffered the consequences of it, and you confessed it. God has forgiven you. Now, forgive yourself, and trust God to work out His purposes in your life. Only God can take a man's two greatest sins and build a temple out of them. I don't understand how God works all things together for good, but He does.

So we can see the three steps we need to take if we want to be set free from the past. First, *accept God's forgiveness.* Just believe the Word of God— that God has forgiven you of all your trespasses. He has cast your sins into the depths of the sea (see Mic. 7:19). They are behind His back (see Isa. 38:17). They are remembered against you no more (see Heb. 10:17). As far as the east is from the west, he has removed your transgressions from you (see Ps. 103:12). Accept God's full and free forgiveness.

Second, *forgive others.* If you're harboring anything against anybody else, confess it to God, and confess it to them if necessary. It will set you free. The greatest freedom in the world is the freedom of forgiveness. This business of having family squabbles and misunderstandings so that you don't talk to people is foolish and sinful. Paul wrote to the Philippians: "Forgetting those things which are behind" (3:13). It is terrible to be living in the past when you ought to be living for the future. Forgive others.

Finally, *forgive yourself*. Quit being so proud. You're no better than any other person. God knows your frame; He remembers that you are dust (see Ps. 103:14). Don't try to drive the memories of sin out of your mind. Just turn them into praise and prayer. Just pray, "Lord, I know I shouldn't have said that. When I think about what I did, it bothers me. But I'm committing it to You now, and I'm going to praise You because I know You are going to bring something good out of it. Thank You for forgiving me." Turn those thoughts into praise and prayer as Paul did. Be a faithful servant of Jesus Christ, and trust the abundant grace of God to see you through.

Many people are being crucified between two thieves—the fears of tomorrow and the regrets of yesterday—and they cannot enjoy today. If you are in bondage to your past, turn it over to Jesus Christ. He is the God of your yesterdays, your todays and your tomorrows, and He will set you free.

Chapter 9

Freedom From Things

Let's think together about the problem of worry and how to be set free from bondage to things. I think this is one of the greatest needs Christians have today—to be delivered from things. We live in a world saturated with things. How easy it is for us to get attached to things and to be controlled by things.

Christians don't like to admit that they worry. They call it being "burdened" or being "concerned," but worry is what it really is. Jesus dealt with this problem in Matthew 6:19-34, a familiar passage. "Lay not up for yourselves treasures upon earth, where moth and rust doth corrupt, and where thieves break through and steal, but lay up for yourselves treasures in heaven, where neither moth nor rust doth corrupt, and where thieves do not break through nor steal; for where your treasure is, there will your heart be also. The lamp of the body is the eye; if, therefore, thine eye be healthy, thy whole body shall be full of light. But if thine eye be evil, thy whole body shall be full of darkness. If, therefore, the light that is in thee be darkness, how great is that darkness!

"No man can serve two masters; for either he will hate the one, and love the other; or else he will hold to the one, and despise the other. Ye cannot serve God and money. Therefore, I say unto you, Be not anxious for your life, what ye shall eat, or what ye shall drink; nor yet for your body, what ye shall put on. Is not the life more than food and the body than raiment? Behold the fowls of the air; for they sow not, neither do they reap, nor gather into barns, yet your heavenly Father feedeth them. Are ye not much better than they? Which of you by being anxious can add one cubit unto his stature? And why are ye anxious for raiment? Consider the lilies of the field, how they grow; they toil not, neither do they spin, and yet I say unto you that even Solomon, in all his glory, was not arrayed like one of these. Wherefore, if God so clothe the grass of the field, which today is, and tomorrow is cast into the oven, shall he not much more clothe you, O ye of little faith? Therefore, be not anxious saying, What shall we eat? or, What shall we drink? or, With what shall we be clothed? For after all these things do the Gentiles seek. For your heavenly Father knoweth that ye have need of all these things. But seek ye first the kingdom of God, and his righteousness, and all these things shall be added unto you. Be, therefore, not anxious about tomorrow; for tomorrow will be anxious for the things of itself. Sufficient unto the day is its own evil."

The English word "worry" comes from an Old Anglo-Saxon word that means "to strangle." The Greek word translated "being anxious" or "being

75

troubled" in the Bible means "to be pulled apart." Worry is dangerous. It will strangle you physically, emotionally and spiritually. It will pull you apart. It can create all kinds of problems, and the only person who can control it is the Christian himself. You and I must determine that things are not going to master our lives. One major cause of worry in our lives is our concern about things, our bondage to things. One of the evidences that we are getting all wrapped up in things is that we worry about them. If we want to have peace, we must learn how to be free from things. Jesus shared several truths with us that will help us to enjoy freedom from things.

It Is Not Wrong to Own Things

First of all, our Lord made it clear that *it is not wrong to own things.* In Genesis 1:31 we read: "And God saw every thing that he had made, and, behold, it was very good." It is not wrong to own things for several reasons.

God Made Things That Are Good

To begin with, *God made things.* In this universe there is God, there are people, and there are things. God is to be worshiped, people are to be loved and served, and things are to be used. God made things, and He did not make anything that is wrong. Things can be used in the wrong way, but they are not sinful in themselves. God made them.

Second, Genesis 1:31 states that *everything God made was good.* In fact, the verse tells us that it was *very* good. So God made things and things are good.

God Knows We Need Things

Third, *God knows that we need things.* "For your heavenly Father knoweth that ye have need of all these things" (Matt. 6:32). We don't need everything, but we do need basic things.

I was in a restaurant recently, waiting to be seated, and a young family came in. The father and mother and two little boys had to wait with the rest of us to be seated.

The younger of the two boys saw a candy machine that contained suckers. The little boy began to jump up and down and cry and hit his mother and say, "I want a sucker! I want a sucker!" Of course, his mother and father were very embarrassed because this is not the way little boys are supposed to act. (I was a little surprised they did not do something about it, but that's another sermon.) This little boy wanted *things,* and he was determined to get them even if he had to upset the entire restaurant and embarrass his mother and father.

Life is not measured by things. When a person dies, someone may ask, "How much did he leave?" He left *everything!* Life is not measured by things. "Take heed, and beware of covetousness; for a man's life consisteth not in the abundance of the things which he possesseth" (Luke 12:15). Mark Twain said, "Civilization is a limitless multiplication of unnecessary necessities." We get all wrapped up in things.

77

God Wants Us to Enjoy and Use Things

Fourth, *God wants us to enjoy things.* First Timothy 6:17 says, "Charge them that are rich in this age, that they be not highminded, nor trust in uncertain riches but in the living God, who giveth us richly all things to enjoy." God wants us to enjoy things. He made things. They are good, and it is not wrong to enjoy them.

Finally, *God wants us to use things.* In First Timothy 6:18 Paul said that we should do good, be rich in good works, be ready to distribute and be willing to share. We should not only *enjoy* things, but we should *employ* things for the good of others and for the glory of God.

Here, then, are five reasons why it is not wrong to own things. God made things. Things are good. We need things. God wants us to enjoy things, and we can use things for the good of others and for the glory of God.

It Is Wrong for Things to Own Us

Our Lord gave us a second truth: *It is wrong for things to own us.* Things are marvelous servants but terrible masters. Matthew 6:21 says, "For where your treasure is, there will your heart be also." *Your heart* can start to love things. The word for this in the Bible is "covetousness." Covetousness means that we must have more things, bigger things, greater things. Then we start to measure life by things. It is possible for your heart to get wrapped up in things. When this happens, you start worrying because your heart gets divided. You get pulled apart.

It is possible for *the mind* to get all wrapped up in things. Matthew 6:22,23 says, "The lamp of the body is the eye; if, therefore, thine eye be healthy, thy whole body shall be full of light. But if thine eye be evil [defective], thy whole body shall be full of darkness. If, therefore, the light that is in thee be darkness, how great is that darkness!"

If your mind is fixed on things, then things will control you and the inner man will get darker and darker. Christ was talking here about conscience. Your conscience is like a window that lets the light into your inner man. As that window gets dirtier and dirtier, less light comes in, and then the light turns into darkness. If I allow my mind to get wrapped up in things, if my outlook is only on things, it will lead to inner darkness.

Things can control your *heart*. "Where your treasure is, there will your heart be also" (v. 21). Things can control your *mind*. Things can also control your *will*. "No man can serve two masters; for either he will hate the one, and love the other; or else he will hold to the one, and despise the other. Ye cannot serve God and money" (v. 24).

A divided life is a destroyed life. If you start living for things, things will become your master, and this will destroy your life. Worry is the evidence that the mind, the heart and the will are possessed by things. That's why our Lord said in verse 25, "Therefore, I say unto you, Be not anxious for your life, what ye shall eat, or what ye shall drink; nor yet for your body, what ye shall put on. Is not the life more than food and the body than raiment?" Our Lord Jesus was saying, "When you start living for things and looking for things and loving things, your inner man starts to deteriorate, and the evidence of this is anxiety. Don't be anxious about your life." "Which of you by being anxious can add one cubit unto his stature?" (v. 27). You can't grow taller by worrying. Instead, worrying will shorten your life. "Therefore, be not anxious saying, What shall we eat? or, What shall we drink? or, With what shall we be clothed? For after all these things do the Gentiles [the lost] seek."

Worry is an evidence of unbelief. Unbelief is an evidence of disobedience. Disobedience is an evidence that something is wrong on the inside. What is wrong? Your heart, mind and will are possessed by things. It is not wrong to own things, but it is wrong for things to own us.

Perhaps you've heard about the Quaker who was watching his wealthy neighbor move in. As you know, the Quakers believed in simplicity of life. The Quaker watched as the movers carried in a great deal of furniture and all sorts of knickknacks and different furnishings. Finally, the Quaker called his neighbor over and said, "Neighbor, I would have a word with thee." The neighbor asked, "What is it?" The Quaker replied, "Neighbor, if ever thou dost think that thou dost need something, come to see me—and I will tell thee how to get along without it!" That is a good philosophy. It leads us to our third instruction.

God Must Be the Master

God must be the master of everything in our lives.

The secret is Matthew 6:33: "But seek ye first the kingdom of God, and his righteousness, and all these things shall be added unto you." In other words, take things out of the *center* of your life, and let God put things where they really belong. When things become your master, life becomes cheap. When things become your master, life is divided, life is defeated. But when Jesus Christ is your Master, then everything in your life finds its proper place, and you start putting the proper price tags on the "furniture" of life. I fear that some people are paying a great price for the cheap things that possess them. Think of the energy and time that is spent on all of the "things" that are so important to you. And yet you may be losing your children, your friends, perhaps even your husband or wife. There are people in hospitals today who would give everything they own to get their health back, and yet many of them are in the hospital because they are living for things. They are worrying, being pulled apart, being strangled by the incessant drive for things. God must be the Master of everything in our lives.

What does it mean to seek first the kingdom of God and His righteousness? It means that God is first in our lives. First thing in the morning, we turn to God in prayer and worship. We turn to Him in the Word. The first day of every week we are in church. The first thing in our lives—the most important thing—is to please Him. When God is first and we are worshiping Him and not things, then people and things fall into their proper place.

Not only do we seek God, but we submit to Him—to His rule and to His righteousness. We are saying, "My Lord and my God!" We are not running our own schedule; we are letting God run our schedule. It is marvelous when God liberates you from the tyranny of things! You can read the newspapers and see all the advertisements and not feel like you have to own all those things. When your neighbor has something that may be more expensive or more showy than what you have, it doesn't bother you at all. You are learning how to be content with what you have. Instead of complaining about what you *don't* have, you are rejoicing about what you *do* have.

All of this takes faith. You have to trust Him to meet your needs. "But seek ye first the kingdom of God, and his righteousness [His rule and His righteousness], and all these things shall be added unto you" (v. 33). This is God's promise. Not *half* of these things, not *some* of them, but "all these things shall be added unto you." David said, "I have been young, and now am old; yet have I not seen the righteous forsaken, nor his seed begging bread" (Ps. 37:25).

I want to warn you that worry can affect you mentally, physically, emotionally and spiritually. It will make you upset and uptight. You will not be able to be the husband, the wife, the worker, the pastor, the son, the daughter you ought to be. Give the whole thing to the Lord! Say, "From now on, I'm going to put Jesus Christ first in my life and seek to please Him. I'm going to submit to God every day— to His rule and His righteousness. I'm going to live to please Him, and I'm going to trust His promise that He will supply all the things I need."

If you want to be free from things, you must understand and obey certain truths. First of all, it is not wrong to own things. Second, it is wrong for things to own us. Third, God must be the Master of everything. Jesus said we should learn to live a day at a time. "Be, therefore, not anxious about tomorrow; for tomorrow will be anxious for the things of itself. Sufficient unto the day is its own evil" (Matt. 6:34). Live a day at a time. A day at a time submit to God and seek God. A day at a time let God give you the things that you need. Whatever He doesn't give you isn't worth having. My prayer is that each of us will learn the real value of things in relation to the spiritual value of life. Don't put the wrong price tags on the things of life. God will supply all of your needs according to His riches in glory (Phil. 4:19), if you'll just seek Him first and submit to Him.

Chapter 10

Future Freedom

As Christians, we enjoy freedom *now,* but our greatest experience of freedom will take place in the future when Jesus returns. The Bible calls this "the glorious liberty of the children of God." Romans 8:18-23 is the key passage:

"For I reckon that the sufferings of this present time are not worthy to be compared with the glory which shall be revealed in us. For the earnest expectation of the creation waiteth for the manifestation of the sons of God. For the creation was made subject to vanity, not willingly but by reason of him who hath subjected the same in hope. Because the creation itself also shall be delivered from the bondage of corruption into the glorious liberty of the children of God. For we know that the whole creation groaneth and travaileth in pain together until now. And not only they, but ourselves also, who have the first fruits of the Spirit, even we ourselves groan within ourselves, waiting for the adoption, that is, the redemption of our body."

Contrast Between Suffering and Glory

The Apostle Paul presented in this passage a

series of contrasts between the present and the future. The first contrast is in verse 18—*the contrast between suffering and glory.* "I reckon that the sufferings of this present time are not worthy to be compared with the glory which shall be revealed in us." Creation was good. God looked on everything He had made and said it was very good. But today it is a *groaning* creation. Suffering occurs everywhere. One day it shall be a *glorious* creation. The pattern that God has established in this world is suffering and then glory. We see it in nature. During the autumn and the winter seasons, in many parts of the world, you can see the suffering and the groaning. But then glory follows in the spring, the summer and the harvest. This was true in the life of our Lord Jesus Christ—first the suffering and then the glory. In I Peter this theme is repeated over and over again—first the suffering and then the glory. The disciples wanted the glory without the suffering. The Devil will give you the suffering without the glory. But the Christian life means first the suffering, then the glory. God has established this pattern.

God's purpose for this world from the beginning was that of glory. Then sin came in and brought suffering. In Romans 5 Paul explained how the fall of the first man brought sin, suffering, death and condemnation into the world. But we have in Jesus Christ the assurance of future glory. Paul expressed this same truth in II Corinthians 4:16-18: "For which cause we faint not; but though our outward man perish, yet the inward man is renewed day by day. For our light affliction, which is but for a moment,

85

worketh for us a far more exceeding and eternal weight of glory, while we look not at the things which are seen, but at the things which are not seen; for the things which are seen are temporal, but the things which are not seen are eternal."

The outward man is perishing. We are growing older, and more and more decay is setting in. But the inward man is being renewed day by day. We are becoming more and more like Jesus Christ. Our affliction is light and only for a moment when compared with the eternity of the glory that lies before us when Jesus comes. Today we are experiencing suffering, but in that future liberty of the children of God, there will be glory.

Contrast Between Expectaton and Manifestation

In Romans 8:19 is a second contrast—*expectation and manifestation.* "For the earnest expectation of the creation waiteth for the manifestation of the sons of God." Another way of saying this is "For the anxious longing of the creation waits eagerly for the revealing of the sons of God." All of nature is eagerly anticipating the return of Jesus Christ. All of nature is on tiptoe, eagerly expecting His return. That's more than we can say for some Christians. Some Christians live day after day as though Jesus never died and as though He were never coming back again. But nature is waiting, expecting the coming of our Lord Jesus Christ. The picture here is that of eager expectation, a person straining, standing on tiptoe, looking for that future hope.

Contrasted to expectation is *manifestation*. All of creation is waiting for the sons of God to be manifested. The word translated "manifestation" in verse 19 is the same Greek word that is translated "revealed" in verse 18. It is the same word that is used in the name of the Book of the Revelation. A time will come when the sons of God are going to be revealed. Today the world cannot see what we really are. The glory that God has put within us and the glory that God has given to us have not been revealed. "Beloved, now are we the children of God, and it doth not yet appear what we shall be" (I John 3:2). We do know that when Jesus Christ returns, we are going to enter into this wonderful glory, "the glorious liberty of the children of God" (Rom. 8:21).

In verse 17 Paul mentioned our inheritance. "If children, then heirs—heirs of God, and joint heirs with Christ—if so be that we suffer with him, that we may be also glorified together." Jesus Christ has already been glorified. We are in Christ; therefore, we have the assurance of future glory. We are joint-heirs—whatever He inherits, we inherit. Jesus prayed to his Father, "Father, I will that they also, whom thou hast given me, be with me where I am, that they may behold my glory, which thou hast given me" (John 17:24). Today is a time of expectation, but when Jesus returns, it will be *manifestation*. God is going to be glorified when His Church is without spot or wrinkle or blemish, when we have been transformed and share His eternal glory.

Contrast Between Vanity and Hope

In Romans 8:20 we have a third contrast: *a contrast between vanity and hope.* "For the creation was made subject to vanity, not willingly by reason of him [God] who hath subjected the same in hope." The word "vanity" means "futility, aimlessness." In the Old Testament it is the name Abel. Adam and Eve named their son "Abel," which means "vanity." You find the words "vanity" and "vanities" 38 times in Ecclesiastes. "Vanity of vanities; all is vanity" (1:2). It's the word for "breath" and "vapor."

There seems to be no reason for what is going on in this world. If you read the newspapers and listen to the news, you say, "What in the world is going on?" It all seems so vain and so futile. But in contrast to the seeming vanity of this creation, we have a blessed hope in Jesus Christ. God has subjected creation to His control. He is working out His plan, and this plan involves hope. Hope in the Bible is not "hope so." It is not like the little boy or girl who is hoping to get a bicycle for Christmas. It is not similar to anything the world is hoping for. Rather, our hope is a certainty. It is the blessed assurance of the future, and this assurance controls the present. God has a plan for this world, and this plan will be carried out.

We have a living hope. "Blessed be the God and Father of our Lord Jesus Christ, who, according to his abundant mercy, hath begotten us again unto a living hope by the resurrection of Jesus Christ from the dead, to an inheritance incorruptible, and undefiled, and that fadeth not away, reserved in heaven for you" (I Pet. 1:3,4). Today the world is subjected to vanity, but when Jesus returns, we will experience the fulfillment of this blessed hope, "the glorious liberty of the children of God" (Rom. 8:21).

Contrast Between Bondage and Liberty

In Romans 8:21 we have a fourth contrast: the contrast between *the bondage of corruption and the liberty of God's children*. "Because the creation itself also shall be delivered from the bondage of corruption into the glorious liberty of the children of God." Now we know why all of creation is waiting for Jesus to come back: Creation cannot be delivered until *we* are delivered! Creation cannot experience glory until *we* experience glory! This is why all creation is waiting for the Creator to return. This is why the Church is waiting for the Redeemer to return.

Creation is in bondage. Because of sin creation is under subjugation (v. 21). Creation will be delivered. Delivered from what? From bondage. What kind of bondage? The bondage of corruption, the bondage of decay. The law of sin and death is operating in nature. There is death, and death leads to decay. Out of that decay comes soil, and from that soil comes life, and the cycle repeats itself: life, death, decay. Your body is subject to the law of sin and death. If we should die, our bodies will turn to dust. When Jesus returns, we shall receive a glorified body.

We cannot break this cycle of life and death. It seems as though every spring, creation is struggling to try to bring forth something new, something that will last. Then autumn comes, and what was brought forth does not last. It dies and decays. One day we shall go to heaven where there is no death, no decay, no corruption, no defilement. We are going to an inheritance that God has prepared for us.

Contrast Between Groaning and Redemption

This leads to the final contrast: the contrast between *groaning and redemption* (Rom. 8:22,23). "For we know that the whole creation groaneth and travaileth in pain together until now" (v. 22). Creation is groaning, groaning in travail like a woman giving birth to a child. In the springtime creation travails to bring forth something new, and then it decays and dies, just as in previous years. "And not only they, but ourselves also, who have the first fruits of the Spirit, even we ourselves groan within ourselves" (v. 23). We don't groan just because of our arthritis, rheumatism, headaches and troubles. Even unsaved people can groan because their bodies hurt! We are groaning within ourselves, *waiting for Jesus to come*. We are groaning for glory. All of creation is groaning for glory, and you and I as Christians should be groaning for glory.

We have "the first fruits of the Spirit" (v. 23). That means we have the down payment of glory in our hearts. We know we are going to heaven because the Holy Spirit lives in our hearts. God said, "Here is the down payment. The Holy Spirit is My earnest, My assurance to you that one day I'm going to take you to heaven and that you shall share in My glory." We will have glorified bodies, bodies like Christ's glorious body. We will no longer face death and decay or all the pain and suffering of this life. We will enjoy "the glorious liberty of the children of God" (v. 21).

Romans 8:30 affirms that we have *already* been glorified. "Moreover, whom he did predestinate, them he also called; and whom he called, them he also justified; and whom he justified, them he also glorified." It doesn't say He *will* glorify us but that He already *has* glorified us. Then what are we waiting for? We are waiting for the *manifestation of that glory*. We are waiting for our adoption, the redemption of our bodies. Our inner man has already been redeemed, but the body has not yet been redeemed. One of these days the body will be redeemed, and our salvation will be complete.

What does this say to us as Christians? For one thing, we know that suffering is not forever. Suffering will be forever for the unsaved. If you don't know Jesus as your Saviour, be prepared to suffer forever. You ought to trust the Saviour now and be delivered from the law of sin and death. "The sufferings of this present time are not worthy to be compared with the glory which shall be revealed in us" (v. 18).

People today hurt and weep. They have difficulties and trials of one kind or another. Let's do what all nature is doing: Let's lift up our hearts and eagerly anticipate the coming of Jesus!

All of the vanity of life will one day be replaced by the fulfillment of hope. The bondage of corruption will be replaced by the glorious liberty of the children of God. The groaning will be replaced by the adoption, the redemption of our bodies. What a wonderful day it will be when Jesus Christ returns and takes us to heaven and shares His eternal glory with us!